Piano · Vocal · Guitar

#1 COUNTRY SONGS OF THE 80's AND 90's

As Listed On The Billboard Hot Country

D0858902

HL Hal Leonard Publishing Corporation
7777 West Bluemound Road P.O. Box 13819 Milwaukee, WI 53213

ISBN 0-7935-0493-7

ABOVE AND BEYOND

Words and Music by
HARLAN HOWARD

Well, I'll give you___ love that's a-

bove___ and be-yond the call of love,_____ and I'll___

nev - er ev - er make __ you cry. ___

Yes, I'll give you __ love that's a - bove __ and be -

yond the call of love _____ and love's some - thin'

To Coda

that mon - ey can't buy. _____

{ Well, a
  We

COME FROM THE HEART

Words and Music by SUSANNA CLARK
and RICHARD LEIGH

come from the heart ___ if you want it to work ___

D.S. al Coda

Now

8

CHAINS

Words and Music by BUD RENEAU
and HAL BYNUM

gives me an - y slack, but if I ev - er break a - way, I'm nev - er com - in' back to these
heart be - gins to sink when I know that all your do - in's tak - in' up an - oth - er link in these

chains, chains, __ shac - kles and chains. __ No mat - ter what it takes, some - day __

__ I'm gon - na break these __ chains, chains, __ shac - kles and chains. __ These

love tak - in', heart break - in', cold hard lone - ly mak - in' chains.

To Coda

You chains.

Love was nev-er meant to be a one way street. _ I was nev-er meant to be

fall-in' at your feet. You got me where you want me and I don't know what to do. You

don't be-long to me, but I ___ be-long to you and these ___ chains.

Chains, chains, ___ shac-kles and chains. ___ No mat-ter what it takes some-day ___

___ I'm gon-na break these ___ chains, chains, ___ shac-kles and chains. ___ These

love tak-in', heart break-in', cold, hard, lone-ly mak-in' chains. Oh, _____

COME NEXT MONDAY

Words and Music by K.T. OSLIN,
RORY MICHAEL BOURKE and CHARLIE BLACK

COULD I HAVE THIS DANCE

Words and Music by
WAYLAND HOLYFIELD and BOB HOUSE

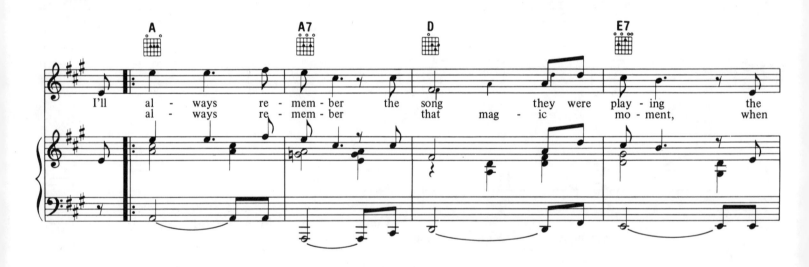

I'll al- ways re- mem- ber the song they were play- ing, the
al- ways re- mem- ber that mag- ic mo- ment, when

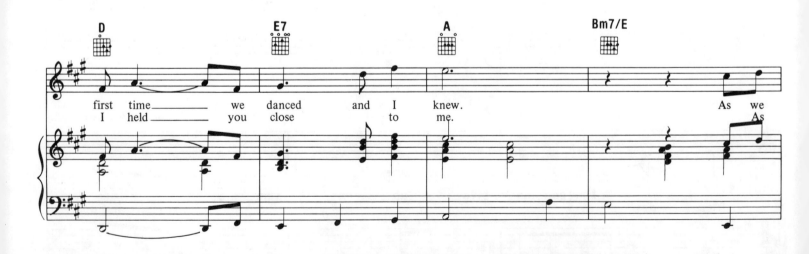

first time _____ we danced and I knew.
I held _____ you close to me.

As we
As

COWARD OF THE COUNTY

Words and Music by ROGER BOWLING
and BILLY EDD WHEELER

Ev - 'ry - one__ con - sid - ered him__ the cow - ard of __ the coun - ty, __

He'd nev - er stood_ one sin - gle time to prove the coun - ty wrong. _

His ma - ma named_ him Tom - my, the

folks just called him yel - low, ___ But some-thing al - ways

told me they were read - in' Tom - my wrong. ___

He was on - ly ten ___ years old ___ when his dad - dy died ___ in pris - on, ___

I looked af - ter Tom - my 'cause he was my broth - er's son. ___

27

(Spoken) there was three of them! (Sung) Tom-my o - pened up___ the door___ and

saw his Beck - y cry-in', The torn dress, the

shat-tered look___ was more than he___ could stand. He

reached a-bove___ the fire - place and took down his dad-dy's pic - ture.

let 'em have it all.___ When Tom-my left_ the bar - room not a

Gat - lin boy was stand-in', He said, "This one's__ for Beck - y." As he

watched the last one fall. *(Spoken) And I heard him say,* "I prom - ised you, Dad,___ not to do

_____ the things you done, I walk a - way from trou - ble when I can.___

DON'T WE ALL HAVE THE RIGHT

Slow waltz (♩ ♩ played as ♩³♪)

Words and Music by
ROGER MILLER

DON'T YOU EVER GET TIRED
(OF HURTING ME)

Moderately

Words and Music by
HANK COCHRAN

You make my eyes run

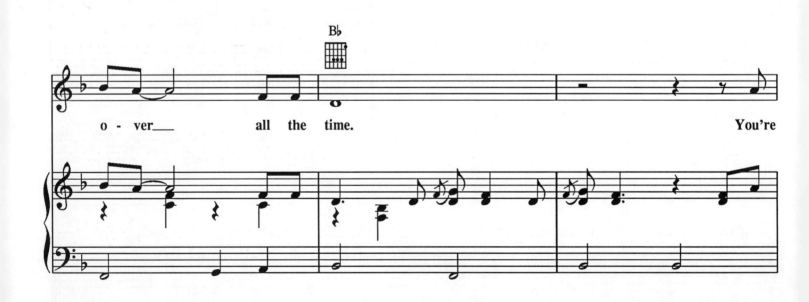

o - ver___ all the time. You're

You _____ must

D.S. al Coda

CODA

Don't you ev - er get tired_____ of hurt - ing

me?_____

FAMOUS LAST WORDS OF A FOOL

Words and Music by DEAN DILLON
and REX HUSTON

FRIENDS IN LOW PLACES

Words and Music by DEWAYNE BLACKWELL
and EARL BUD LEE

FOREVER AND EVER, AMEN

Words and Music by DON SCHLITZ
and PAUL OVERSTREET

Lively Country

You may think that I'm talk-in' fool-ish,
makes you've heard that I'm wild and I'm free.

time takes its toll on a bod-y,
makes a young gi-rl's brown hair turn gray.

MCA MUSIC PUBLISHING

- ther, as long as old wom - en sit and

talk a - bout___ old___ men; if you won - der how long___

___ I'll be faith - ful

(I'll be
well just

hap - py to tell___ you a - gain.___
lis - ten to how___ this song ends;

I'm gon-na love___ you for- ev -er and ev - er, for -

ev - er and ev - er, a - men.

They say

I WOULDN'T HAVE MISSED IT FOR THE WORLD

Words and Music by KYE FLEMING,
DENNIS MORGAN and CHARLES QUILLEN

1. Our paths may nev-er cross_ a-gain;_
2. (see additional lyrics)

may-be my heart_ will nev-er mend,_

but I'm glad for all the good_ times. You brought me so_

Verse 2.
They say that all good things must end.
Love comes and goes just like the wind.
You've got your dreams to follow,
But if I had the chance tomorrow,
You know I'd do it all again.
(To Chorus)

GRANDPA
(TELL ME 'BOUT THE GOOD OLD DAYS)

Medium Slow Country

Words and Music by
JAMIE O'HARA

(sung 8va lower)

Grand-pa, tell me 'bout the good old days.__
Grand-pa, ev-'ry-thing is chang-in' fast.__

Some-times __ it feels __ like this world's gone cra-
We call __ it prog - ress, but I just don't know.__

HOLD ME

I'VE COME TO EXPECT IT FROM YOU

Words and Music by DEAN DILLON
and BUDDY CANNON

1. So up-set,
2. A mil-lion times,
3. Instrumental
4. I could raise hell,

A nerv-ous wreck. can't be-lieve____ you said good-bye.
A mil-lion lines____ and I bought 'em ev-'ry-one.
But what the hell,____ it would-n't do a bit____ of good.____

I'VE CRIED MY LAST TEAR FOR YOU

Words and Music by CHRIS WATERS
and TONY KING

When you left me lone-ly here,___ I
Used to lay a-lone in bed,___

thought that I___ would drown in tears.___ As one was
with my pil-low soak-ing wet.___ All of those

IN A LETTER TO YOU

Words and Music by
DENNIS LINDE

I tore my let-ter up. I could-n't e-ven start to
took the morn-ing sun peek-ing through the trees and the
In a day or two, just you wait and see, you're

tell you what's real-ly here in my heart.___ There's on-ly so much that
dan-de-lion silk tan-gled in the breeze.___ I fold-ed 'em up and I
gon-na get a spe-cial de-liv-er-y.___ You'll know the way I feel. There

words can say___ so I sent you a piece of this beau - ti - ful day.
sealed 'em with a kiss. It's the kind of let - ter that you can't re - sist. } Oh, I want _
can't be an - y doubt when you o - pen it up and let the love spill out.

___ you to know that I took a rain - bow _ and sent it off in a let - ter to you. _

___ I took some flow - ers in the spring and made a sweet clo - ver ring __ and sent it

IT AIN'T NOTHIN'

Words and Music by
TONY HASELDEN

My boss is the boss
It was writ-ten all ___

-'s son, ___ and that makes ___ for a real ___ long day. ___
o-ver her face ___ she was a-bout ___ to climb ___ the walls. ___

D.S. (Instrumental)

When that day is fi-nal-ly done ___ I'm fac-ing
She said, "You got-ta get me out-ta this place, ___ 'cause e-ven

IT'S JUST A MATTER OF TIME

Moderately

Words and Music by CLYDE OTIS,
BROOK BENTON and BELFORD HENDRICKS

I'M NO STRANGER TO THE RAIN

Words and Music by SUNNY CURTIS
and ROD HELLARD

I've fought with the dev - il, _____ got down on his lev - el. But I ne - ver gave in so he gave up on me. I'm no strang - er to the rain. I can spot bad weath - er, _____ and I'm

LIVING PROOF

Words and Music by JOHNNY MacRAE
and STEVE CLARK

LOVE WITHOUT END, AMEN

Words and Music by
AARON G. BARKER

NEXT TO YOU, NEXT TO ME

Words and Music by ROBERT ELLIS ORRALL
and CURTIS WRIGHT

LOST IN THE FIFTIES TONIGHT
(IN THE STILL OF THE NIGHT)

Words and Music by MIKE REID,
TROY SEALS and FRED PARRIS

Additional Lyrics

These precious hours, we know can't survive.
Love's all that matters while the past is alive.
Now and for always, till time disappears,
We'll hold each other whenever we hear:

SONG OF THE SOUTH

Words and Music by
BOB McDILL

all picked the cot - ton but we nev - er got rich.
we were so poor____ that we____ could - n't tell.____
coun - ty got the farm and they moved to town.

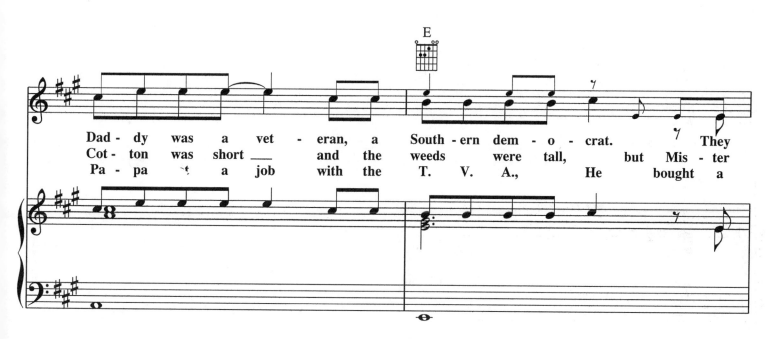

Dad - dy was a vet - eran, a South - ern dem - o - crat. They
Cot - ton was short___ and the weeds were tall, but Mis - ter
Pa - pa 't a job with the T. V. A., He bought a

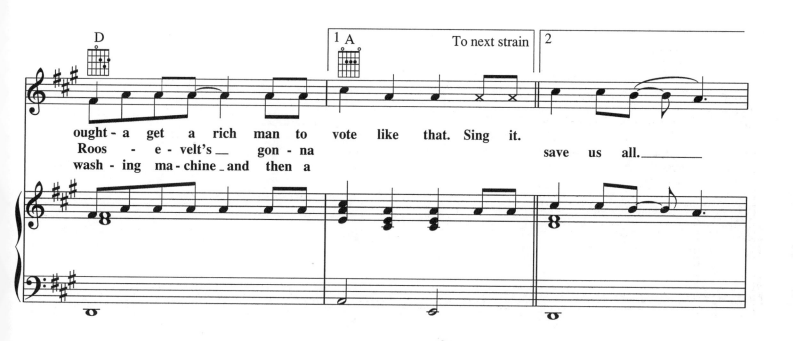

ought - a get a rich man to vote like that. Sing it.
Roos - e - velt's___ gon - na save us all._____
wash - ing ma - chine _ and then a

1 A   To next strain   2

Well back a - gain.

D.S. al Coda
CODA
A
Play it.
Song,
E
D
song of the South.
A
E
D
Gone, gone with the wind.
A
E
Song, song of the South.

ON SECOND THOUGHT

Words and Music by
EDDIE RABBITT

sec - ond thought, ___ I'll just turn a - round ___ here in my tracks ___

and walk ___ back ___ in - to your arms ___ where I be - long. ___

I was wrong. On sec - ond thought,

I a - pol - o - gize ___ for what I've done, ___ 'cause you're the on -

- ly one__ I'll al - ways be in __ love with.

Yes, you're the on - ly one__ I'll al -

- ways be in ____ love _____

a - with. _____

SET 'EM UP JOE

Moderately (played as)

Words and Music by DEAN DILLON, BUDDY CANNON,
HANK COCHRAN and VERN GOSDIN

STAND BY ME

Words and Music by BEN E. KING,
JERRY LIEBER and MIKE STOLLER

TURN IT LOOSE

With a steady beat

Words and Music by DON SCHLITZ,
BRENT MAHER and CRAIG BICKHARDT

Some call it coun-try with a lit-tle bit of rhy-thm and blues.
feel like danc-in' and you just can't stay in your seat.

And when the
Your

boys start rock-in' there's a beat that you just can't lose.
knees start knock-in' and you can't help stomp-in' your feet.

144

put on your shout - in' shoes_____ and turn it loose,_____

and turn it loose._____

You

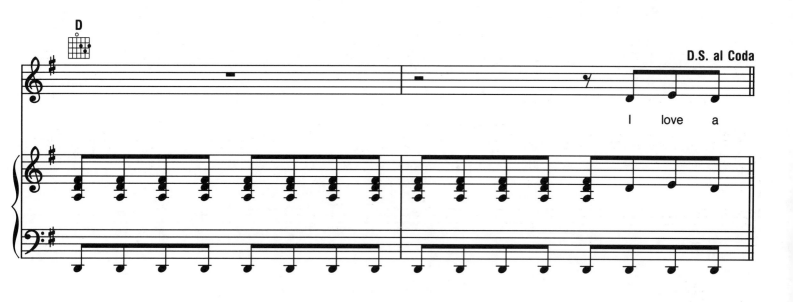

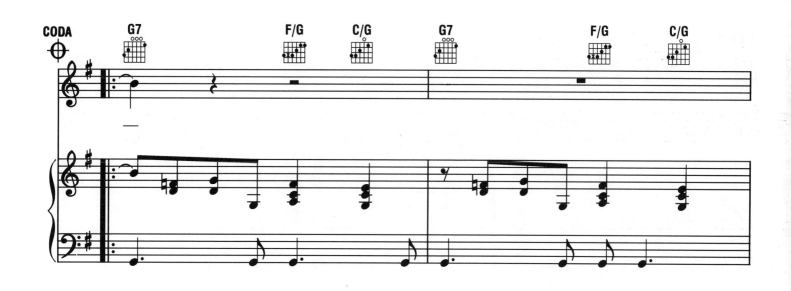

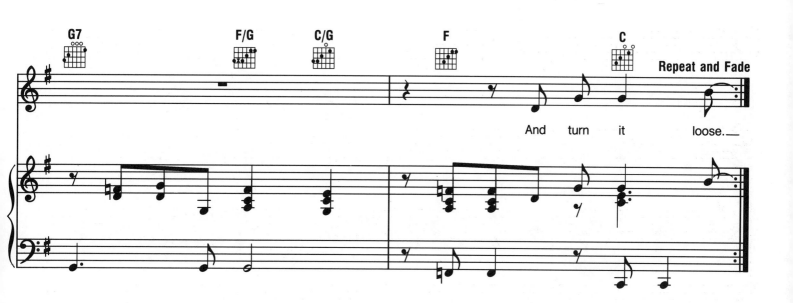

TO ALL THE GIRLS I'VE LOVED BEFORE

Lyric by HAL DAVID
Music by ALBERT HAMMOND

TIMBER I'M FALLING IN LOVE

Words and Music by
KOSTAS

1. The right time,_____ the right place._____
2.,D.S. Who knows _____ how love starts._____

The right bod - y,_____ the right face._____
I woke up_____ with_____ you_____ in my_____ heart._____

WHO'S LONELY NOW

Moderate Country two beat

Words and Music by KIX BROOKS
and DON COOK

You walked out on a
I feel a whole lot

good love._____ You found some-bod-y new._____
bet-ter._____ I've got a new at-ti-tude._____

158

When you're re - ject - ed____ you feel ne -

glect - ed,___ it's true.

In your con -

WE BELIEVE IN HAPPY ENDINGS

By BOB McDILL

And we for-get who's right or wrong;— Then one of us will
and won-der why we're oh, so proud;— When all that mat - ters

end it all,__ with just a smile.)
an - y - how__ is our love.)

We be - lieve in hap - py end - ings, nev - er break - ing,

on - ly bend - ing; Tak - ing time e - nough for mend - ing

YOU LIE

Words and Music by AUSTIN ROBERTS,
BOBBY FISCHER and CHARLIE BLACK

Moderate country waltz

We lie in the dark. ___ I
Des - p'rate to talk, ___
How long un - til ___ you

know you're a - wake. ___ The on - ly sounds ___ are the
yearn - ing to touch, ___ burn - ing in - side ___ 'cause I
just can't go ___ on, and the urge to break ___ loose is

YOU LOOK SO GOOD IN LOVE

Words and Music by KERRY CHATER,
RORY BOURKE and GLEN BALLARD

Your Favorites in
COUNTRY MUSIC
and more...

#1 COUNTRY SONGS OF THE 80'S
44 Chart-topping country hits, including: American Made • Any Day Now • Could I Have This Dance • Crying My Heart Out Over You • Forever And Ever Amen • Forty Hour Week (For A Livin') • Grandpa (Tell Me 'Bout The Good Old Days) • He Stopped Loving Her Today • I Was In The Stream • My Heroes Have Always Been Cowboys • Smoky Mountain Rain • Why Not Me • You're The Reason God Made Oklahoma.
_____00360715 $10.95

80'S LADIES—TOP HITS FROM COUNTRY WOMEN OF THE 80'S
23 songs by today's female country stars including: Roseanne Cash, Crystal Gayle, The Judds, Reba McEntire, Anne Murray, K.T. Oslin and others. Songs include: I Don't Know Why You Don't Want Me • Lyin' In His Arms Again • Why Not Me • A Sunday Kind Of Love • Could I Have This Dance • Do'Ya • Strong Enough To Bend.
_____00359741 $8.95

THE AWARD-WINNING SONGS OF THE COUNTRY MUSIC ASSOCIATION First Edition
All of the official top five songs nominated for the CMA "Song Of The Year" from 1967 to 1983. 85 selections, featuring: Always On My Mind • Behind Closed Doors • Don't It Make My Brown Eyes Blue • Elvira • The Gambler • I.O.U. • Mammas Don't Let Your Babies Grow Up To Be Cowboys • Swingin' • You're The Reason God Made Oklahoma.
_____00359485 $16.95

AWARD-WINNING SONGS OF THE COUNTRY MUSIC ASSOCIATION Second Edition
An update to the first edition, this songbook features 18 songs nominated for "Song of the Year" by the Country Music Association from 1984 through 1987. Songs include: Islands In The Stream • To All The Girls I've Loved Before • God Bless The U.S.A. • Seven Spanish Angels • Grandpa (Tell Me 'Bout The Good Old Days) • On The Other Hand • All My Ex's Live In Texas • Forever And Ever, Amen.
_____00359486 $8.95

THE NEW ULTIMATE COUNTRY FAKE BOOK
More than 700 of the greatest country hits of all-time. Includes an alphabetical index and an artist index! Includes: Cold, Cold Heart • Crazy • Crying My Heart Out Over You • Daddy Sang Bass • Diggin' Up Bones • God Bless The U.S.A. • Grandpa (Tell Me 'Bout The Good Old Days) • Great Balls Of Fire • Green, Green Grass Of Home • He Stopped Loving Her Today • I.O.U. • I Was Country When Country Wasn't Cool • I Wouldn't Have Missed It For The World • Lucille • Mammas Don't Let Your Babies Grow Up To Be Cowboys • On The Other Hand • Ruby, Don't Take Your Love To Town • Swingin' • Talking In Your Sleep • Through The Years • Whoever's In New England • Why Not Me • You Needed Me • and MORE!
_____00240049 $35.00

THE BEST COUNTRY SONGS EVER
79 all-time country hits, including: Always On My Mind • Could I Have This Dance • God Bless The U.S.A. • Help Me Make It Through The Night • Islands In The Stream • and more.
_____00359135 $14.95
_____00359134
Plastic-comb Bound $17.95

COUNTRY VOLUME 1 —ULTIMATE SERIES
100 top country hits made popular by some of today's biggest recording artists, featuring: Another Sleepless Night • Blessed Are The Believers • The End Of The World • Every Which Way But Loose • Heartbreaker • Honky Tonk Blues • Hopelessly Devoted To You • Lay Down Sally • Let's Do Something Cheap And Superficial • Mountain Love • Ruby, Don't Take Your Love To Town • Stand By Me • Through The Years • Walking The Floor Over You • The Women In Me • Your Cheatin' Heart • more.
_____00361400 Spiral Bound $19.95
_____00361401 Perfect Bound $16.95

COUNTRY VOLUME 2—ULTIMATE SERIES
100 more giant hits: Could I Have This Dance • I.O.U. • Islands In The Stream • Nobody Likes Sad Songs • Any Day Now • Daytime Friends • Flight 309 To Tennessee • Highway 40 Blues • I Always Get Lucky With You • I Wouldn't Have Missed It For The World • I Think I'll Just Stay Here And Drink • Kentucky Rain • Smokey Mountain Rain • Somebody's Gonna Love You • You Put The Beat In My Heart • You're The First Time I've Thought About Leaving • many more.
_____00361402   Spiral Bound $19.95
_____00361403   Perfect Bound $16.95

THE GREAT AMERICAN COUNTRY SONGBOOK
The absolute best collection of top country songs anywhere. 70 titles, featuring: Any Day Now • Could I Have This Dance • Heartbroke • I Was Country When Country Wasn't Cool • I'm Gonna Hire A Wino To Decorate Our Home • It's Hard To Be Humble • Jambalaya • Smokey Mountain Rain • Through The Years • many others.
_____00359947 $12.95

HL• Hal Leonard Publishing Corporation
For more information, see your local music dealer, or write to:
P.O. Box 13819 Milwaukee, Wisconsin 53213

Prices subject to change without notice.   Prices may vary outside the U.S.A.
Some products may not be available outside the U.S.A.

COUNTRY STANDARDS
A collection of 51 of country's biggest hits, including: (Hey Won't You Play) Another Somebody Done Somebody Wrong Song • By The Time I Get To Phoenix • Could I Have This Dance • Daddy Sang Bass • Forever And Ever, Amen • Bless The U.S.A. • Green, Green Grass Of Home • Islands In The Stream • King Of The Road • Little Green Apples • Lucille • Mammas Don't Let Your Babies Grow Up To Be Cowboys • Ruby Don't Take Your Love To Town • Stand By Me • Through The Years • Your Cheatin' Heart.

_____00359517 $10.95

COUNTRY MUSIC HALL OF FAME
The Country Music Hall Of Fame Was Founded in 1961 by the Country Music Association (CMA). Each Year, new members are elected—and these books are the first to represent all of its members with photos, biography and music selections related to each individual.

Volume 1
Includes: Fred Rose, Hank Williams, Jimmie Rodgers, Roy Acuff, George D. Hay, PeeWee King, Minnie Pearl and Grandpa Jones. 23 songs, including: Blue Eyes Crying In The Rain • Cold, Cold Heart • Wabash Cannon Ball • Tennesse Waltz.
_____00359510 $8.95

Volume 2
Features: Tex Ritter, Ernest Tubb, Eddy Arnold, Jim Denny, Joseph Lee Frank, Uncle Dave Macon, Jim Reeves and Bill Monroe. Songs include: Jealous Heart • Walking The Floor Over You • Make The World Go Away • Ruby, Don't Take Your Love To Town • Kentucky Waltz • Is It Really Over • many more.
_____00359504 $8.95

Volume 3
Red Foley, Steve Sholes, Bob Wills, Gene Autry, Original Carter Family, Arthur Satherley, Jimmie Davis, and The Orginal Sons Of The Pioneers. 24 songs: Peace In The Valley • Ashes Of Love • San Antonio Rose • Tumbling Tumble Weeds • Born To Lose • Worried Man's Blues • many more.
_____00359508 $8.95

Volume 4
Features: Chet Atkins, Patsy Cline, Owen Bradley, Kitty Wells, Hank Snow, Hubert Long, Connie B. Gay and Lefty Frizzell. Song highlights: Crazy • I'm Sorry • Making Believe • Wings Of A Dove • Saginaw, Michigan • and 16 others.
_____00359509 $7.95

Volume 5
Includes: Merle Travis, Johnny Cash, Grant Turner, Vernon Dalhart, Marty Robbins, Roy Horton, "Little" Jimmie Dickens. 19 selections: Sixteen Tons • Folsom Prison Blues • El Paso • Mockingbird Hill • May The Bird of Paradise.
_____00359512 $7.95

9/89